The Fabulous Book of Feminist Fairy Tales

THE FABULOUS BOOK OF FEMINIST FAIRY TALES

Written by A . L . Brooks
Illustrated by Sophie Gabriel

Copyright © 2017 A. L. Brooks

ISBN-13: 978-1545016572
ISBN-10: 1545016577

This book is dedicated to all the amazing women in my life. Most importantly: my Mother Rachael, my Nana Margaret, and my Jamjar Anita. Thank you for showing me how to be a strong female. I only hope that all other women around the world are lucky enough to have role models like yourselves.

CONTENTS

Introduction 12

Originally by 'The Brothers Grimm'
Rapunzel 13
Rumplestiltskin 14
Snowy White 17
The Frog Prince 19
Twelve Dancing Princesses 20

Originally by 'Charles Perrault'
Cinderellie (Cinderella) 23
Sleeping Beauty 24

Originally by 'Hans Christian Anderson'
The Little Mermaid 27
The Princess and the Pea 28

Originally by 'Gabrielle-Suzanne Barbot de Villeneuve'
Beauty and the Beast 30

INTRODUCTION

Hi! You are about to read a book based on the fairytales from an array of authors. At the time of writing the original tales, women were seen as inferior and stereotyped as weak and beautiful creatures, they were also rarely clever. I grew up with these original tales, as I'm sure many of you who are reading this did also. I wanted to write this book to not only update the tales, but to mirror what is going on in the world currently. My aim was to make stories where women were at the forefront of the action and they were taking control of their lives rather than focusing on men. Enjoy the stories and illustrations in this book, and whether you are male or female, young or old, I hope together we can reach equality of all things in the near future.

                                                    Happy reading.

                                                    A. L. Brooks

RAPUNZEL

There was once a man called James and a woman called Rachael. The pair loved each other very much. For some time now they had been wanting a child. They tried and tried for years, but could not succeed. Finally, a miracle appeared to happen, and Rachael became pregnant.

The home that the couple lived in, overlooked a garden which was full of the most beautiful fruit and vegetables. However, the garden belonged to a powerful witch. Everyone was scared of this witch and so the townspeople all bullied her. Wanting to be left alone, the witch locked herself in a large tower, only coming out to tend to her garden.

At this moment in history, there was a worldwide strawberry shortage, and every day the pregnant Rachael pleaded with her boyfriend to find her some strawberries to settle her hormonal cravings. James knew that the witch had strawberries, so one night he climbed over the garden wall and picked some of the fruit. Weeks passed and Rachael had finally given birth to a beautiful baby girl called Alisia. In the dead of night, the witch, seeking revenge, crept into the bedroom where Alisia slept and stole her from her cradle. The witch kept Alisia in her tower, never to see her parents again.

Rachael and James had mourned for the loss of their child for 20 years. Alisia had grown, as children often do. She was now a beautiful young woman, with hair a hundred metres long for it had never been cut. She was no longer called Alisia, as the witch had changed her name to Rapunzel in order to hide her identity.

One day whilst the witch was in her garden, Rapunzel was watching a TV documentary called, "The mysterious case of Alisia." A picture of Alisia as a baby came on the screen. She had a birthmark, shaped like a strawberry on her face- the same mark as Rapunzel. The documentary then displayed a picture of the parents house, which Rapunzel recognised as the neighbours. "I'm the lost baby." She thought. She tied the end of her hair to the bed and quietly abseiled down the tower cutting her hair with the garden scissors. She ran to the house next door and was reunited with her family. The police were called and the witch was given 20 years in prison. Alisia desperately wanted to put her life with the witch behind her. So, she shaved her head happily and donated all her hair to 'The Little Princess Trust'.

RUMPLESTILTSKIN

Once there was a postman who was poor, but who had a beautiful daughter. The postman had been invited to speak to the king, and due to nerves and wanting to seem important he told the King, "My daughter, Maggie, can spin straw into gold." The king was amazed and asked him to bring his daughter to the palace, so he could see it for himself.

The next day the King took Maggie into a room which was full of straw, gave her a spinning-wheel, and said, "If you don't spin this straw into gold, your father will be put to death for lying to the King." The King gave her till morning. She had no idea how straw could be spun into gold, and she began to cry. But all of a sudden she heard a strange voice "why are you crying?" Maggie looked up to see an unusual looking man. She told the man what was wrong. The man bargained with Maggie and said he would do it in return for her necklace.

In the morning the king arrived and was delighted with Maggie. So delighted, he demanded that she do it another 2 times. And each time the man appeared, he would offer to help her in return for something valuable. The last time he spun the straw into gold, he demanded her first born child. Maggie was helpless, so she agreed. Finally the King set her free.

Afterwards, the Kings son. He had come round asking to see her and apologising for his fathers actions. They went on many dates, and eventually they fell in love and married. Years passed but Maggie had still not had a child. The strange man grew impatient and knocked on her door. When she answered, a dog leaped out from behind Maggie. He jumped on the man and licked his face furiously. Maggie and the Prince laughed. "Rumple, get down and go back inside!" The strange man was incredibly angry and asked Maggie "Why haven't you had a child yet? I've been waiting for 10 years!" To which maggie responded, "We decided we didn't want children, so we got a dog instead." And with that, Maggie slammed the door in his face.

SNOWY WHITE

Once upon a time in a faraway kingdom, a girl was born. Her complexion was as white as snow, her lips were as red as blood, and hair as dark as the night sky. This child was named Zoe, but due to her fair complexion, everyone called her Snowy. Zoe's parents were the King and Queen, making her a Princess. A few months passed and a sadness fell on the kingdom as the Queen had died.

A year later, the King remarried a beautiful woman, but she extremely arrogant, and she hated anyone that she thought might be more physically attractive than her. She had a magic mirror that would always speak the truth. One day, when the Princess had turned 18, the Queen asked the magic mirror, "Who is the most beautiful woman in the world?" The mirror replied, "The Princess Zoe, as she is as beautiful on the inside as she is out." A rage came over the Queen and she started to treat Zoe very unkindly. Zoe knew she deserved to be treated better so moved out of the castle.

She had seen an advertisement in the local newspaper for a room available in a large house in the woodland area. She responded to the advertisement and had finally found a new place to live. Her 7 housemates were shocked at Zoe's amazing height (6ft 1", to be precise), which made them all feel like dwarves. Zoe still wanted more from life, so even though she was rich due to her mothers inheritance, she applied for a job as a marketing assistant at a health magazine called, 'The Red Apple'. The happy ending? She got the job.

THE FROG PRINCE

Back when the world was young, and the humans and the animal people could speak to each other, there was a young girl called Lucy who would find comfort in speaking to animals. She spent her whole childhood playing with the rabbits and birds in her back garden.

The girl eventually became a woman, and at the age of 29 years old, she was invited to a friends 30th birthday party. It was fancy dress themed birthday party and Lucy always won the award for best fancy dress. She decided to go as a Princess and made her costume from scratch. Lucy was very talented at making things.

On the night of the party Lucy went outside into the garden for some fresh air. She could hear the birds in the trees all talking. Many of them complimented her outfit. But then she heard a different voice, a deep, croaky voice. She turned around and on a small table there was a frog, puckering his lips. "My darling Princess, I may look like a frog but I promise you, I am a prince, kiss me and you shall see!" Lucy immediately said, "No." She couldn't think of anything worse than kissing a frog. But the frog kept pushing and demanded that Lucy kiss him. Lucy became increasingly more angry, "Didn't anybody ever teach you that no means no? You must respect peoples choices. Now leave me alone." The frog hopped away and accepted defeat. Lucy went back inside for another drink and enjoyed the rest of her night, hassle free.

TWELVE DANCING PRINCESSES

Once upon a time there lived a King and Queen, who were very happily married. So happily married that they had twelve children, all girls. Sometimes they struggled to remember all their daughters names, but they were called: Alice, Bethany, Charlotte, Dannielle, Emma, Francesca, Georgia, Hannah, Imogen, Joanna, Keira, and Lydia. Because of the King and Queens' awful memory, they would sing the alphabet whenever they were looking for their children. A for Alice, B for Bethany- you get the idea.

The Kingdom was going through dark times. Dancing had been forbidden in the Kingdom after the King had an embarrassing fall at his birthday, which landed him in the emergency room at the local hospital. Despite this, his twelve daughters all had a secret love of dancing. They would often sneak out of their rooms at night to go to local dances. They especially loved to dance to the song 'ABC' by 'The Rackdaughter 4'.

However, one early evening, the King knocked on his youngest daughter's door to ask about the school parents evening. He knocked the door several times, but there was no answer from the other side. The king tried to open the door but it was locked. He grew increasingly suspicious of his children. He decided to hire a detective. Hard times had fallen on the kingdom since the recession, so instead of money, he offered the detective one of his daughters to marry. However, the detective was very wise and he told the King that women were not property and that he should try to talk to his daughters rather than spy on them. The daughters decided to be honest with their father and told him that they were sneaking out of the kingdom to go dancing. At first the King was angry, but after a while he softened and realised he was being too harsh by not letting them dance. The king decided he wouldn't let his fear of falling get in the way of his daughters passions. He put on a huge ball for the kingdom and happiness was restored.

CINDERELLIE

Once upon a time, there lived a man and his daughter called Elinor. They lived in a large beautiful house. Sadly a few years before, the mans wife- and Elinor's mother, died. This was something that was very upsetting to Elinor- but she always remembered the lessons that her mother taught her. The main one? Always stand up for what you believe in.

A few years passed. Elinor was now 16. Her father felt something was missing in his life and his daughter's. He decided to remarry. The woman he married was a very beautiful woman with two daughters. The woman was kind and treated Elinor as if she was her own daughter. Years later, Elinors father needed to go on a business trip out of town. He walked down the stairs to leave the house but was suddenly gripped by excruciating pain down his left shoulder and chest.

Weeks passed by very quickly. Elinor was struggling to come to terms with her fathers passing. She tried to be strong, but her stepmother was extremely upset, as this wasn't the first time she had lost a husband. She would take it out on Elinor. She would make her do all the housework, her daughters would have lovely days to the spa and bully Elinor by calling her names. One day, Elinor was doing the housework and had become dirty from cleaning the fireplace. They laughed at her and nicknamed her Cinderellie. Soon Elinor had had enough. She lectured her stepmother on not pitting women against each other. 'We need to support each other, not make each other feel worse than we already do.' She would say. Her stepmother realised she was being unreasonable and apologised to Elinor.

Some time later, the household was invited to a royal ball, the stepmother bought them all lovely dresses and thought that the ball would be a great opportunity to make them all feel better. At the ball, Elinor caught the eye of the Prince. He asked to dance with her to which she accepted. However, whilst they were dancing the Prince kept making comments about her feet, which made Elinor feel sick. She left the Prince to dance with other people and lived happily ever after with her stepmother and sisters.

SLEEPING BEAUTY

Once, long ago, in a little Kingdom that lay in the midst of high hills and wide forests, a King and Queen had a baby girl called Lauren. The whole country rejoiced in this happy news and the King and Queen had a huge party to celebrate. They invited all the fairies except one, the fairy called Molly. Rumour has it that the King was against her coming to the party because he didn't want his child seeing someone who was not attractive by societies standards.

Each fairy that attended the party gave the Princess Lauren a gift with their magic. The first fairy gave the Princess a love of knowledge. The second, great health and strength. The third, a beautiful singing voice. Suddenly, the fairy Molly appeared at the party in a powerful rage. This was not a good time of the month for Molly. She was so angry at not being invited to the party that she put a curse on the Princess: "On her 15th birthday she will prick her finger on the spindle of a spinning wheel, and on that night she will go to bed and die in her sleep!"

Five minutes later she returned to the party realising that she had overreacted. She knew that Lauren was not to blame for her father's prejudice. Instead, she put a spell on the King so that he could only see the beauty that exists inside women rather than valuing their physical attributes.

THE LITTLE MERMAID

Down in the depths of the Baltic Sea, there was a huge castle. In this castle lived the King of the Sea. The king had many beautiful daughters, who all treasured their father and were very obedient. All, but one. His youngest daughter, Millie, was a curious little Princess who wished to explore the land of the people above. However, Sea law prohibited her from going up to the surface until she was 16, though many argued the law should be changed to 18.

Her 16th birthday came along very quickly, and Millie was more excited than she'd ever been in her entire life. She swam up to the surface in record time. She erupted through the water and had her first breath. She could smell the salt in the air and sea. She couldn't believe her eyes. All the colours of the land above were so peaceful. Swirls of blues and greens danced together all around her. A large wooden object floated on the surface nearby, she understood that this was a boat. She could hear laughter coming from it.

She moved closer and closer to the boat until she saw land people. If the land was beautiful then there were no words to describe the people that lived on it- especially one of them. Her heartbeat quickened and she thought to herself, "I want to spend the rest of my life with this handsome man." She paused for a moment, remembering that she hadn't even spoken to this man. She realised that she was being insane and went back home immediately to study for her SeaCSE's.

THE PRINCESS AND THE PEA

A long time ago, in a very rich Kingdom called Blueditch, a Queen was desperate for her son to marry. However, the Prince also had very high standards and nobody was ever good enough for him. He had many demands: "She must be able to cook, clean, give me many children, be beautiful at all times, be able to sing and dance and do yoga, she must be four inches shorter than me and have ginger hair. But most importantly, she must be a Princess."

One day a storm happened and by coincidence, the Princess Lily from the Kingdom of Tahp was travelling through Blueditch and was looking for shelter- not because she couldn't handle a bit of rain, but because she had just had her hair freshly coloured and didn't want the colour to run and stain her clothes. She decided the Castle would be a good place to stay. She knocked on the door, and the Prince answered.

The prince being incredibly shallow was dazzled by her freshly done hair. His mother realised that this girl might be the one! She asked her son, "Why don't you marry this girl?" (because apparently it's just that easy). But the prince decided to try and test the Princess. He placed a pea under 20 mattresses and told the Princess that she must sleep on top of them. She obviously couldn't feel the pea whilst she was sleeping, so the Prince told the Queen, "She's not good enough to marry me." Luckily, the Princess Lily overheard the Prince's statement, and responded with, "Firstly, I would never marry someone like you anyway. Secondly, I'd like to see you feel a pea underneath 20 mattresses." She swiftly left the Kingdom of Blueditch and never looked back.

BEAUTY AND THE BEAST

In a small but beautiful village in northern France lived a young girl called Sophie. Sophie was known throughout the village as being very beautiful. But Sophie knew there was more to life than looks, like books! Sophie had read every book in the village and was fluent in multiple languages.

One day, Sophie's father went missing. Sophie decided to retrace her fathers steps and went out to look for him. She came across a scary looking castle and noticed her fathers horse nearby. She knocked on the door of the castle but no one would answer. She bravely went in and repeatedly called out for her father. He responded shakily "leave quickly, before he comes and gets you." However, Sophie was not afraid and carried on looking for her father, following his voice until she found him, trapped behind bars.

All of a sudden a gravelly, booming voice came from behind Sophie. "Who are you?" The angry voice shouted. Sophie became furious very quickly and demanded that the voice release her father. The voice came into the light. It belonged to a huge terrifying beast. Sophie threatened the beast with contacting the police for wrongful imprisonment. The beast decided he was no match for Sophies brains and that it was in his best interests to let the father and daughter duo go. Sophie went on to live a happy life as a lawyer.

Printed in Great Britain
by Amazon